Making Books
by Hand

A STEP-BY-STEP GUIDE

Acknowledgments
We would like to thank the owners of Rugg Road Paper Company,
Casandra McIntyre, Drew Ellis, and Amy Madanick,
as well as the staff at Rockport Publishers.

First published in the United States of America by:
Quarry Books, an imprint of
Rockport Publishers, Inc.
33 Commercial Street
Gloucester, Massachusetts 01930-5089
Telephone: (508) 282-9590
Fax: (508) 283-2742

Distributed to the book trade and art trade in the United States by:
North Light, an imprint of
F & W Publications
1507 Dana Avenue
Cincinnati, Ohio 45207
Telephone: (800) 289-0963

Other distribution by:
Rockport Publishers, Inc.
Gloucester, Massachusetts 01930-5089

ISBN 1-56496-328-4
10 9 8 7 6 5 4 3 2
Designer: Beth Santos Design
Printed in Hong Kong
Materials and project photography by Martin Berinstein
Cover photography by Kevin Thomas and Martin Berinstein
Additional photography by Martin Berinstein (pp. 6, 9, 89, 98–99); Martin Berinstein and Guido Piacentini (pp. 96–97);
    Kay Canavino (pp. 102–103); David Caras (p. 91); and Kevin Thomas
Quilters and Weavers (p. 89) and *Rhythms* (p. 98) appear courtesy of the Department of Prints and Graphic Arts, Houghton
    Library, Harvard University
Handmade marbled paper on pages 64–65, 68–73 © Alan Pendley, Aqualina, Inc., Petaluma, California
Kaleidoscope paper on cover and on pages 1, 8, 9, 30, and 31 used with permission of Langdell Paperworks
Marbled paper on cover © Talin Book Bindery
Purple handmade paper on cover © Zina Papers
Poem on page 16 by Emmett Manna

Making Books by Hand

A STEP-BY-STEP GUIDE

Mary McCarthy
Philip Manna

Quarry Books
Gloucester, Massachusetts
Distributed by North Light Books
Cincinnati, Ohio

Contents

Introduction

When you use the term *book*, do you think of an object with a front and back cover and pages in the middle? We all know what a book is. Yet this narrow definition limits our imaginations. Let's expand our concept of *book*.

Must a book have covers? If the covers do not open, is it still a book? What about content—can a book be a book without words or pages? And do the pages have to be paper? Can the contents be objects rather than text or pictures? Must the contents be bound? Does a book have to lie flat? What if you could eat it? (Binders often use only materials that are safe enough to eat.)

For me a book is an object that opens and closes. It is a vessel with content that can be transported. It is personal and tactile in both the making and the viewing. A book needs to be touched, turned, and looked at in different ways over time. It is made to establish a relationship with the viewer. A book can be experienced intimately by one person or viewed collectively by a large audience.

Mary McCarthy
Rhythms

I have been an artist and an art teacher for more than twenty years. After my first son was born in 1982, the responsibilities of motherhood and teaching full-time left little time for my art. As I struggled to reconcile my conflicts,

I discovered that the process of making books fit well with my fragmented life of mother, artist, and teacher. I began to use the short pieces of my day to make the separate pieces of my books.

As a teacher, I believe there is a bookmaker in all of us. We all have stories to tell, materials and images to collect, and information to record. Making books by hand using traditional methods does not have to be difficult. In the pages that follow, you will find directions to make a variety of books using tools found around your home or at local art and hardware stores.

Professional bookbinders use presses, cutters, sewing frames, and other specialized tools for stamping and finishing, which are all necessary for a bindery producing books and boxes of great quantity and/or complexity. In *Making Books by Hand*, we will keep it simple, yet help you make professional-quality products. The most important thing to remember is to explore and have fun.

Mary McCarthy

About Paper

The projects described in this book are made using a variety of papers. When selecting specific papers for a project, ask yourself the following questions: Is the paper appropriate for the book's purpose? Does the paper help express the look or feel you want your book to have? Does the paper complement the other materials used in the book? Finally, ask the people working at paper stores and art stores for advice. They are usually quite knowledgeable and will be glad to help.

While modern technology has made it possible to produce mass quantities of paper cheaply, there are still papers being made around the world by hand using natural fibers and old-world techniques. These decorative papers work well as covers, end sheets, or even interior pages. Whether machine- or handmade, papers vary in thickness, texture, color, and weight. A visit to a local paper store or a well-stocked art store will reveal the tremendous assortment of papers you can choose from. They can be thin enough to see through, such as many Japanese rice papers, or as thick as the cardboard of a corrugated box. They can be as smooth as silk tissue paper or as rough as tree bark.

All paper has one common characteristic—the grain. The grain indicates the arrangement or direction of the fibers. A book will be stronger, less likely to warp, and easier to fold if the grain of all your papers is parallel with the spine. Companies often label which way the grain runs. For machine-made commercial paper, the grain usually runs the length of the paper. If the grain is not listed, you can test it by bending or folding the paper. A piece of paper folds easily and without cracking if the crease is parallel with the grain. If you fold a piece of paper and it shows signs of cracking along the crease, you know the grain runs in the opposite direction. If you still cannot determine which way the grain runs, cut a small piece and wet it. As the paper dries, it will begin to bend in the direction of the grain. For handmade papers, the grain is of less concern. It is arranged in many different directions, and is therefore not as clearly defined as it is in machine-made commercial paper.

Mary McCarthy
Declaration of Love

Materials and Supplies

In addition to various kinds of paper, you will need a few other materials and supplies to complete the projects in this book.

Cloth

Most books use cloth for all or part of the cover. Binder's cloth is a strong, durable cloth with a paper backing. It can be purchased at binderies and paper stores. Other types of cloth can also be used. If the cloth you want has a loose weave or is very thin, it must be backed with paper to give it added strength and provide a surface on which to spread glue. Rice paper makes good backing material.

Adhesives

Cloth and paper are adhered to a book using glue or paste. For the projects described in this book, I use a polyvinyl acetate (PVA). It is white, dries clear, and can be thinned with water. You can substitute PVA with other white paper glues. You can also use wheat paste, rice paste, or paste made from cornstarch. If you want to mix your own paste, you can find recipe books that show you how (see the Suggested Readings at the end of this book).

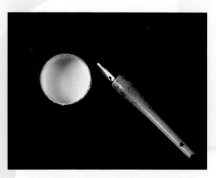

Thread

You will need to sew the bindings on some of the projects in this book. Professional binders use linen thread, which is strong but rather expensive. As a substitute, you can use thick cotton thread, embroidery silk, or even dental floss if the book is small. A variety of ribbons, cords, or twine can add color to your spine. Avoid using sewing thread, which breaks easily.

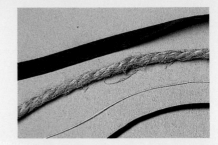

Cover Board or Binder's Board

The front and back covers of most books are made with heavy paper or cardboard. Davy board, a type of cover board used by binders, can be purchased from local binderies or through catalogs (see the list of sources at the end of the book). Cover boards vary in thickness from 0.02 inch (a thin board) to 0.147 inch (a thick board). The latter is almost impossible to cut by hand. For practical purposes, the thickness of your cover boards should be about 0.08 or 0.09 inch, except in cases when a thin board, such as shirt board (0.02), is required.

If you have difficulty finding binder's board, you can use chip board, mat board, or even make your own board by gluing and pressing thin boards or layers of paper together.

Scrap Paper

Making books by hand can get a bit messy. Use large scraps of paper as a barrier to protect your materials and work surface while gluing and cutting. Remember to discard wet barriers and replace them with clean, dry ones. Rolls of wax paper and craft paper wrappers are an inexpensive source of protective paper.

Sandpaper

Medium sandpaper can be used to round any sharp corners or irregular edges of your cover boards.

Damp Cloth

Keep a damp cloth handy while you are gluing. Use it to clean your fingers so that you do not get any unwanted glue on finished surfaces.

Tools

This list includes all the tools you could possibly need to complete every project in this book. Not every tool is required for each project; some call for just a pair of scissors and a bone folder. For other, more complicated, projects, such as the Window-and-Post Album, you will need a hand drill, C-clamps, and screw posts.

1 Hand drill with various bits

2 Bone folder with a round and pointed end

3 Clamps or metal art clips

4 Screw posts

5 Square angle rule

6 Assorted craft needles

7 Pencil

8 Hole punch (optional)

9 Needle tool

10 Awl (optional)

11 Glue brush

12 Scissors

13 Utility knife or mat knife

14 Beeswax (optional)

15 C-clamps

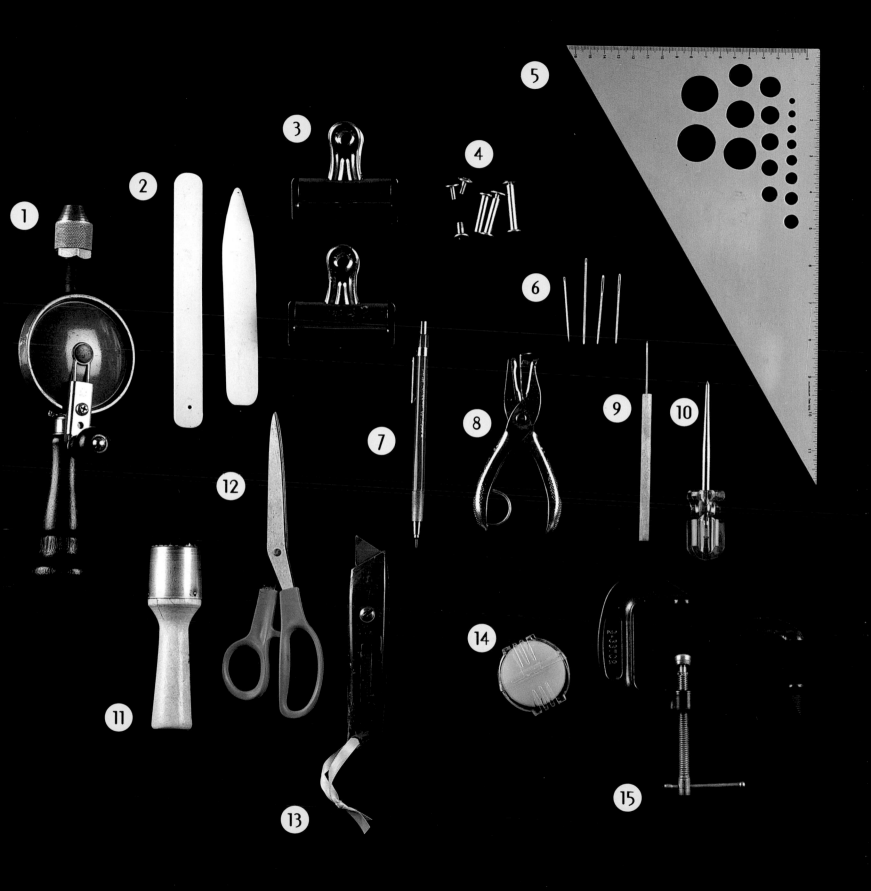

How to Make Corners

For many of the projects in this book, cover boards are wrapped with either cloth or paper. The type of material you use, whether it is thin paper or cloth, thick or brittle paper, or standard cloth or paper, will determine how you wrap the corners of the boards. It requires practice to make neat corners. Take time to study the three methods of wrapping corners described below. For each method, make sure you cut the material no closer than ¼" (.5 cm) to the corners of the board.

Method ONE: *For Thin Paper or Cloth*

Cut off the corners of your material at a diagonal fold, and glue one side of the material down on the board.

Use a bone folder to press the paper down at a slight angle over the corner.

Glue and fold the paper on the adjacent side in the same way.

Method TWO: *For Thick or Brittle Paper*

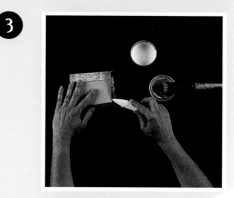

Cut off the corners of your paper at a diagonal fold, and glue one side down on the board. Then, with scissors, cut a straight line from the fold of the cloth that extends to the corner of the board.

With your bone folder or a finger, tuck the small triangular piece you have just created around the corner onto the lip of the adjacent side. Snip off the peak that has formed with scissors as shown.

Glue and fold the adjacent side down on the board.

Method THREE: *For Cloth or Paper*

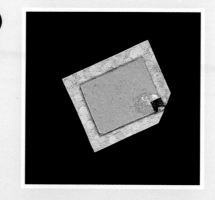

Cut a square into the cloth or paper as shown. Cut carefully so that one corner of the square remains attached to the material.

Glue and fold the square over the inside of the board.

Glue and fold the adjacent sides of the material down on the inside of the board.

An accordion book is ideal for displaying a poem, family portraits, or a scenic panorama of a favorite vacation spot.

Jamaican Dreams

They are my dreams of returning.

Jamaican dreams are Dorchester dreams.
Projects and nice neighborhoods.
Dreams of props and cream.
Colors, black and green.
Many different shades and many different scenes.
You got section 8 and mansions with large gates.
Both places change my state and my fate.

Dorchester or Jamaica is a must.
From French Vanilla to
Chocolate Deluxe.
Either place I lust.
'Cause either place
with cream is enough.

Emmett Manna

Accordion Art Books

Accordion books work well as blank books to write, sketch, or paint in. They emerged from the Orient, where they were traditionally used by Buddhists to keep their sutras or to store calligraphy or paintings. The typical accordion book is made from a single piece of folded paper attached to two covers. The continuous length of paper, unrestricted by binding, is ideal for writing and illustrating a favorite poem. You can paint or write on both sides of the folded page, and use paper of any weight or color that coordinates with your writing or artwork.

Unlike most other books, accordion-style books not only lie flat and compact on a table, they can also stand open for display as a sculpture, or hang, spread out, from a bulletin board or wall. Accordion books made with rigid panels of thick cardboard can hold mounted photos, which, when open, reveal a panoramic view of a favorite vacation spot or vista.

How to Make an Illustrated Poem Book

- You can attach the front and back covers of an accordion book to each other by adhering them to a single piece of cover paper.

- Folding your pages accurately may take some practice. A simple and inexpensive way to acquire this skill is to practice folding a piece of accounting tape. To ensure success, make your first accordion book no more than eight pages long.

- Use a damp cloth or paper towel to quickly wipe up any excess glue that would mar your cloth or paper cover.

When open, this accordion book displays a poem illustrated with watercolor paints. This style of accordion—two hard covers sandwiching a single strip of folded paper—is made up of an even number of pages to allow the front and back covers to point in the same direction when the inside pages of the book are revealed. Sixty-five-pound paper is a good weight to use for the inside sheet because it can be easily folded.

To determine the length of the inside paper needed, multiply the width of the page by the number of pages you want. For example, if you wish to make a mini accordion book that has six pages, 2" (5 cm) wide, you will need to cut a length of paper measuring 12" (30.5 cm). The grain of the paper should run parallel with the folds of the book.

MATERIALS

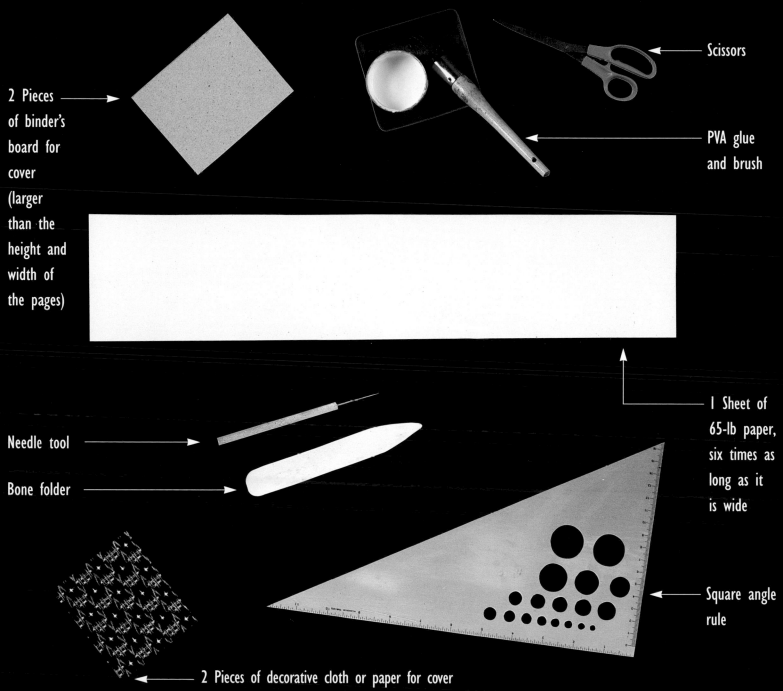

2 Pieces of binder's board for cover (larger than the height and width of the pages)

Scissors

PVA glue and brush

Needle tool

Bone folder

1 Sheet of 65-lb paper, six times as long as it is wide

Square angle rule

2 Pieces of decorative cloth or paper for cover (larger than the height and width of the cover boards)

1

Beginning on the left side of your paper, measure the exact length of one page. Use a needle to make a small hole on the bottom edge of your paper to mark the length. Fold the paper at the hole. Make sure the bottom edges are lined up, then use a bone folder to make a sharp crease. This is your first page.

2

With the first page folded down, take the needle and make a hole in the lower right-hand corner to mark the end of page one. Flip the paper over so the hole is now at the top of your paper, and fold it at the hole. Make sure the top edges are lined up. Use the bone folder to make a sharp crease. This is page two.

3

Repeat this method of folding until you reach the end of the paper.

4

Cut the front and back cover from the binder's board ⅛" (.3 cm) larger than the height and width of your pages. Cut two pieces of cover paper or cloth 1½" (4 cm) larger than the height and width of your boards. Spread a thin coat of glue quickly and evenly over the entire surface of one board.

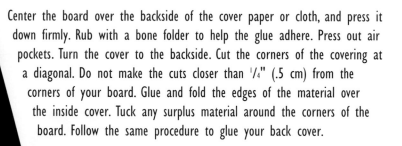

5

Center the board over the backside of the cover paper or cloth, and press it down firmly. Rub with a bone folder to help the glue adhere. Press out air pockets. Turn the cover to the backside. Cut the corners of the covering at a diagonal. Do not make the cuts closer than $1/4$" (.5 cm) from the corners of your board. Glue and fold the edges of the material over the inside cover. Tuck any surplus material around the corners of the board. Follow the same procedure to glue your back cover.

6

Spread glue evenly over the inside of your front cover. Center the first page of your book over the cover, then press it down firmly. Use a bone folder to press out air pockets.

7

Spread glue evenly over the inside of your back cover. Center the last page of your book over the cover, then press it down firmly. Use a bone folder to press out air pockets.

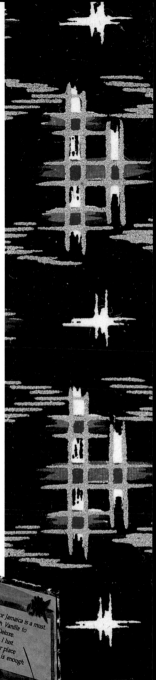

8

To finish the book, decorate the pages using watercolor paints and paper scraps and pasting or writing poems or pictures.

How to Make a Book Panorama

The hard-board accordion, a sturdier version of the Illustrated Poem Book, is perfect for displaying a series of panoramic photos that are mounted on a piece of rigid cardboard. Decorative paper frames the photos on one side and complementary cloth covers the other side.

Use a utility knife to cut the thick pieces of cardboard—do not attempt to cut through the cardboard with one stroke. Instead, hold down a ruler or measuring angle to guide your knife as you make a series of strokes that gradually deepen the cut. To ensure that the book folds together with the four corners of each page meeting, use a square angle rule to cut the corners of each page at a 90 degree angle.

Bits and Pieces

- If you are planning to add materials to your pages, leave extra space between the sections of the book.

- Cut the cardboard pieces on a scrap piece of thick cardboard to save your work surface.

- To conceal the inside edge of the cardboard at the central hinge, don't forget to add two cloth strips to the top and bottom of the hinge, before turning down the top and bottom cloth edges.

- To prevent air bubbles and keep the decorative paper straight as you glue it to the cardboard, press from the center and work outward, toward each end.

MATERIALS

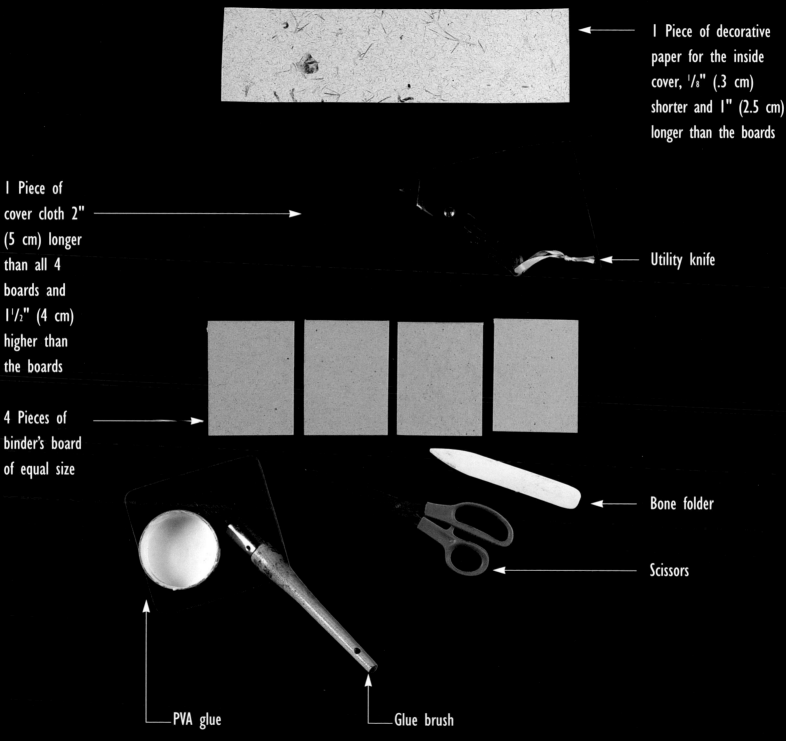

1 Piece of decorative paper for the inside cover, ⅛" (.3 cm) shorter and 1" (2.5 cm) longer than the boards

1 Piece of cover cloth 2" (5 cm) longer than all 4 boards and 1½" (4 cm) higher than the boards

Utility knife

4 Pieces of binder's board of equal size

Bone folder

Scissors

PVA glue

Glue brush

Cut four boards of equal size. Cut cloth for your cover 2"
(5 cm) longer than the combined length of the four boards.
The cloth will be 1½" (4 cm) larger than the height of
your boards, with ¼" (.5 cm) of space between the first and
second, and then the third and fourth boards. Draw a dividing
line from top to bottom in the middle of the cloth. Apply glue
evenly over one side of two boards. Place these boards side by
side on top of the back of the cloth so they meet directly over
the line. Press down firmly.

2

Turn the cloth over. Rub the bone folder over
the entire surface to press out air pockets. These
boards will be your two inside pages.

3

Apply glue over one side of your two remaining boards. Place one board on each side of your inside pages. Leave a space between the inside and outside pages that is equal to two and a half times the thickness of the board—about $^1/_4$" (.5 cm) space, then press them down firmly. Turn the cloth over. Rub the bone folder over the entire surface to press out air pockets.

4

Turn the cloth cover on its backside and snip off the corners by making a diagonal cut with your scissors. Do not cut closer than $^1/_4$" (.5 cm) from the corners of your end pages. Next, make two cuts along the midpoint line (drawn in step 1) that extend beyond the top and bottom where your inside pages meet.

5

From a separate piece of cloth, cut two strips $^1/_2$" x 1" (1 cm x 2.5 cm). Spread glue on the backside of each piece. Fold the two inside pages of your book so they are standing back to back. Place one of these small cloth strips horizontally across the top of the exposed spine and down the sides. Place the other cloth strip horizontally across the bottom of the exposed spine and down the sides. Rub both pieces with your bone folder to help them adhere.

6

Flatten your book out and apply glue along the remainder of the cloth. Fold the cloth around the boards and press it down firmly. Tuck any surplus material around the corners of the page. Use the bone folder to press out air pockets and to fit the cloth into the channel between your inside and outside pages.

7

Cut the piece of paper you have chosen for your inside cover $\frac{1}{8}$" (.3 cm) shorter than the height of your book and 1" (2.5 cm) longer than the length.

8

Spread a thin coat of glue quickly and evenly over the entire surface of your four pages and in the narrow channel between the inside and outside pages.

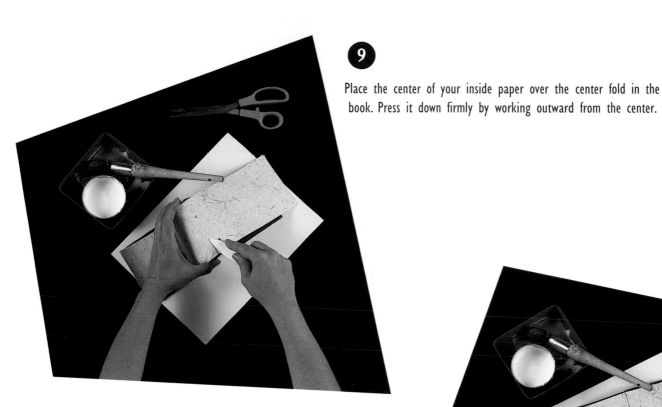

9

Place the center of your inside paper over the center fold in the book. Press it down firmly by working outward from the center.

10

Use the bone folder to press out air pockets and to fit the paper into the channels as shown.

A signature book is perfect for making music booklets, keeping a journal of your garden, or recording reflections in a personal diary. It opens flat and is easy to write in.

Over the weekend my little cousins came into Dorchester from Vermont. We went to the Swan Boats but they are not working anymore. So we went to the park and played on the slides then we got iced cream. Then we walked to the train station got off at our stop and went home. In the morning we all went down to another cousins house where we had a family reunion. At the reunion we played basketball, wrestling, played with cap guns and ate kZorya. So all and all I had a great time.

Eli

Journals *and* Scrapbooks

One of the most effective ways to make a notebook, journal, or scrap-book is to use signatures, one or more pieces of folded paper that have been sewn together at the fold, with or without a cover. Pamphlet books, which are the simplest of these sewn signature books, are fast and easy to make, and lend themselves to homemade music booklets, theater pro-grams, or even menus.

Signature books are ideal for making into journals, where you need to be able to lay the book open, and read or write in one page at a time. They are also well-suited for scrapbooks or travelogues, where photos, inter-spersed with text, are arranged sequentially or chronologically. To make a scrapbook, the signatures can be sewn into a flexible accordion binding, called a *concertina*, that accommodates photographs or other bulky material. Record books and storybooks are some other common exam-ples of signature-style books.

How to Make a Simple Booklet

Bits and Pieces

- The thread you use to fasten the pages to the cover will become one of the book's prominent decorative features —be creative! Use colorful cord, embroidery thread, or thin, $1/8$" (.3 cm) ribbon.

- Use a thick card stock for the cover. Or, to further increase the thickness of the cover, add another layer of cardboard inside the cover board or outside, where you can use the additional layer to decorate the cover.

- To help the thread slide easily through the holes in the spine without tearing the paper, pull it through some beeswax.

If you want to quickly and inexpensively make a large number of small, handmade books, the pamphlet book may be your best option. Think of it as a handmade alternative to the stapled photocopies usually produced for small-scale special events, such as community theater or concert programs.

To make the booklet, you will need a heavy decorative paper for your cover and a lighter-weight paper for your pages. Before deciding on the size and quantity of pages, consider that with this style of book, the pages are formed by folding sheets of paper in half. For example, a single sheet of paper $8^1/2$" x 11" (21 cm x 28 cm) will give you four pages, each $5^1/2$" x $8^1/2$" (14 cm x 21 cm).

Materials

1 Sheet of heavy cover paper $\frac{1}{2}$" (1 cm) larger than the paper used for inside pages

3 Sheets of paper for inside pages

Needle tool

Scissors

Bone folder

Utility knife

Needle and thread

Beeswax

Square angle rule

2 Sheets of decorative end paper $\frac{1}{2}$" (1 cm) smaller than the cover paper

1

Take the sheets of paper you have selected for your pages and fold them in half. Next, separate the sheets and use a bone folder to make a sharp crease in each one. Then fold them back together.

2

Cut the cover paper $1/2$" (1 cm) larger than the height and width of the sheet of paper you folded for the pages. For example, if you are making your pages from a sheet of paper $8^{1}/_{2}$" x 11" (21 cm x 28 cm), cut a cover that is 9" x $11^{1}/_{2}$" (23 cm x 29 cm). Fold the cover in half. Use the bone folder to make a sharp crease.

3

Lay all the pages on top of one another and place them in the center of the cover. Open your book to the center fold. With a needle, jab a hole in the middle of the fold that goes through the pages and cover. Make a second hole in the fold about 1" (2.5 cm) from the bottom and a third hole in the fold about 1" (2.5 cm) from the top.

4

Cut a piece of thread that is two times longer than the height of your book and thread your needle. With your book open to the center fold, carefully turn it over so that the pages remain in place. Take your needle and push it through the middle hole. Pull the thread through until you are left with a 3" (8 cm) tail. Push the needle through the hole at the top of your pages and pull the thread through.

5

Push the needle through the hole near the bottom of your cover and pull the thread through. Push the needle through the hole in the middle of your pages again. Pull the thread through.

6

Take the two tails and pull them together tightly. Tie a knot around the piece of thread that now runs from the top hole of your cover to the bottom hole. Trim the remaining thread to the desired length.

7

Cut two pieces of decorative paper to use for your end sheets ½" (1 cm) smaller than the cover.

8

Spread a thin layer of glue over the side of the paper you do not want showing.

9

Place end sheets inside the covers of the pamphlet. Rub them with a bone folder to remove wrinkles or air pockets.

How to Make a Journal

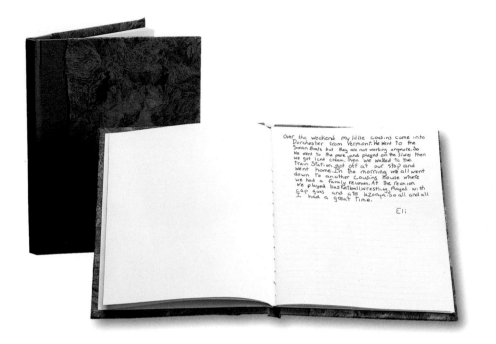

If you want to make a journal or diary that will last longer or be sturdier than a pamphlet book, consider making a hardcover signature book. The folded and sewn sheets of paper from a pamphlet book are glued to a cardboard cover and spine made of binder's board covered in binder's cloth and decorative paper. The piece of cardboard for the spine gives the book a rigid, durable, square-back binding.

The instructions that follow require eight sheets of paper to create a single-signature book of exactly thirty-two pages—the standard length of a children's book. Avoid making books in this style that are longer than thirty-two pages: the holes and pages tend to slip out of alignment.

Bits and Pieces

- A single sheet of paper gives you four pages, so a signature of thirty-two pages requires eight sheets of paper. Make sure you fold the grain of the pages parallel to the direction of the spine.

- Select cover paper and cloth to reflect the contents of your book. For example, to make a garden journal, use petal infusion paper, paper that is made with plants and flowers.

- As you sew together your signature, remember one important rule of book-making: never take your thread over the top or bottom edge of the signature pages.

- To prevent your handmade back from warping, make sure that the grain of all the boards and papers is parallel with the spine, and that, immediately after it is finished, you put the book under pressure for twenty-four hours.

MATERIALS

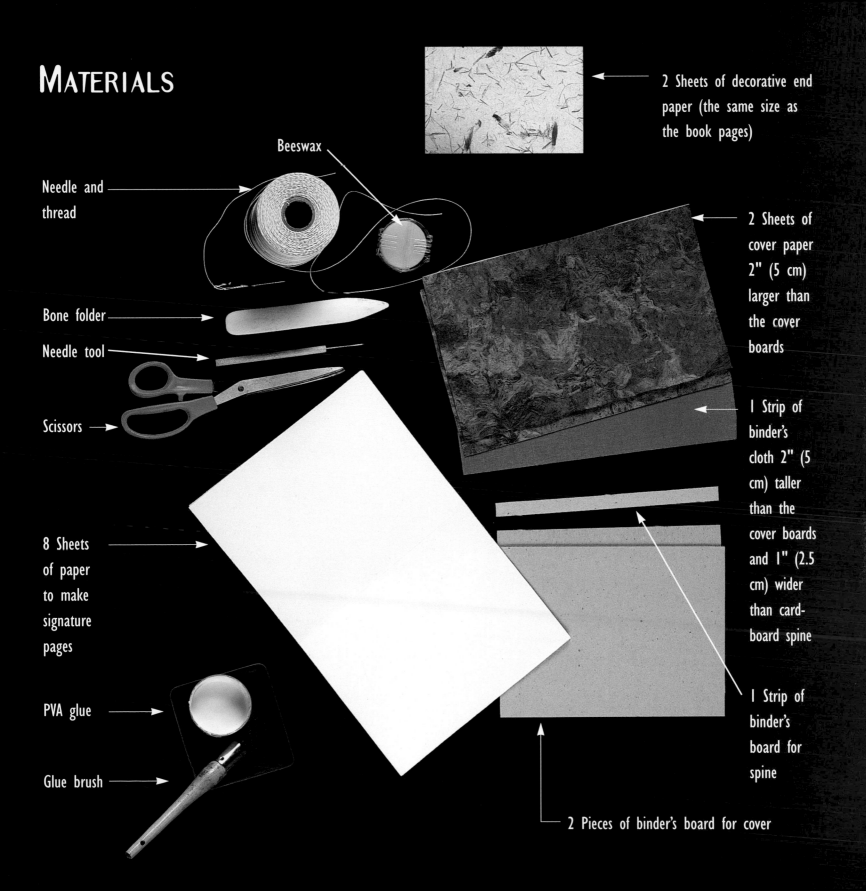

2 Sheets of decorative end paper (the same size as the book pages)

Beeswax

Needle and thread

2 Sheets of cover paper 2" (5 cm) larger than the cover boards

Bone folder

Needle tool

1 Strip of binder's cloth 2" (5 cm) taller than the cover boards and 1" (2.5 cm) wider than cardboard spine

Scissors

8 Sheets of paper to make signature pages

1 Strip of binder's board for spine

PVA glue

Glue brush

2 Pieces of binder's board for cover

1

Take the eight sheets of the paper selected for your pages and fold them in half. Then separate the sheets and use a bone folder to make a sharp crease in each one.

2

Open your pages, stack them one on top of the other at the center fold. With a ruler placed in the fold, start at the bottom and use a needle to jab holes in the crease every $1/2$" (1 cm). Make sure the holes go through all of the sheets.

3

Cut a piece of thread that is twice the height of your book, run it through some beeswax, and thread your needle. With the pages open at the center fold, carefully turn them over so the pages remain in place and the holes are lined up. Push your needle through the bottom hole. Pull the thread through until you are left with a 2" (5 cm) tail. Push your needle through the next hole in the center fold. Pulling the thread taut, weave your way up through the holes to the top hole (do not go over the top edge), then weave back down. The thread will now be filling the empty spaces left during your ascent. When you get back to the bottom hole, tie a knot with the two tails of thread that remain.

4

For your cover, cut two pieces of binder's board ¹/₄" (.5 cm) taller than the height of your pages. The width of the cover should be the same as the width of your pages. Cut a spine from your binder's board ¹/₄" (.5 cm) taller than the height of your pages. The width of your spine should equal the combined thickness of your cover boards and pages. For example, if the thickness of your front and back cover measures ¹/₄" (.5 cm) and the thickness of your folded pages measures ¹/₄" (.5 cm), then the width of your spine should be ¹/₂" (1 cm).

5

Cut a section of binder's cloth that is 2" (5 cm) taller than the height of your covers. The width of your cloth should be at least 1" (2.5 cm) wider on each side of your spine so it can adhere properly to your covers. Center your spine on the cloth vertically and horizontally then make a mark at the top and bottom to indicate the center. Remove the spine and apply glue quickly and evenly over the entire surface of the cloth. Use the marks you made to position your spine in the center of the cloth, then press it down firmly.

6

Place one cover on each side of the spine. Leave a space between the spine and the cover that is two and a half times the thickness of the binder's board. Press both cover boards down firmly.

7

Cut the paper you have chosen for your outside cover 2" (5 cm) taller than the height of your cover boards. Your cover paper should be wide enough to slightly overlap the cloth and wrap around the inside edge of your cover board. Cut two pieces, one for the front cover and another for the back cover. Spread glue over the entire surface of your cover paper, and place it on your front cover board so that it slightly overlaps the cloth. Press the paper down firmly. To make a tight adhesion, rub the entire surface with a bone folder. Look for air pockets and press them out. Follow the same procedure for your back cover.

8

Open your book and snip the four corners of your cover paper at a diagonal. Do not make the cuts closer than ¹/₄" (.5 cm) from the corners of your cover board. Fold the cover paper and cloth over and press it down firmly. Tuck any surplus material around the corners of the cover board. Fold the cloth over at the top and the bottom of the cover.

9

Use the bone folder to press out air pockets and to fit the cloth tightly into the channel between the spine and covers. Place the cover under weights for a few hours while it dries.

10

For your front end sheet, fold a piece of decorative paper that is the same size as your pages. Then, unfold the end sheet and turn it over. Spread a narrow strip of glue along one side of the crease.

Refold the end sheet and place it directly over the front page of your book. Press the glued side down firmly. Repeat to adhere the end sheet to the back page.

11

Place the pages inside your book. Center them so that your cover extends $1/8$" (.3 cm) beyond the top and bottom of your pages. Place a piece of scrap paper under your front end sheet before spreading glue over the surface. Remove the scrap paper and close the front cover. Press the cover down firmly onto the end sheet.

12

Open the front cover and use the bone folder to rub out air pockets or bumps. Follow the same procedure to adhere the end sheet to your back cover. Place your book under pressure for 24 hours to help the glue seal and to prevent your book from warping.

How to Make a Scrapbook

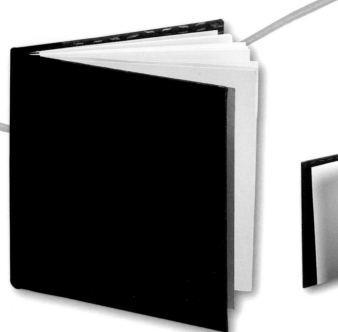

Bits and Pieces

- Make the end sheets and the individual signatures a bit wider than what you actually want for the finished product. After the binding has been sewn together, you can trim your book to the desired width.

- A simple pamphlet stitch fastens the signature to the accordion. See New Directions, where this stitch is used again for How to Make an Extended Accordion.

- You will know if you have sewn the signatures correctly if the shape of the thread through the signatures is a figure eight.

This concertina scrapbook has an accordion binding of folds that makes it easy to add photographs or other bulky material to the pages.

Interior pages can be made of either lightweight text paper or a heavier cover stock. Use heavy cover stock for the accordion-fold binding, which extends to act as the end sheets. To ensure that the end sheet is long enough to cover your pages after you have made the folds, measure cover stock equal to the length of both covers, plus 1" (2.5 cm) for each signature you intend to include in the book.

The finished book will be 6" x 6¼" (15 cm x 15.5 cm) wide. The signature paper should be 5¾" (14.5 cm) high and 13" (33 cm) wide.

MATERIALS

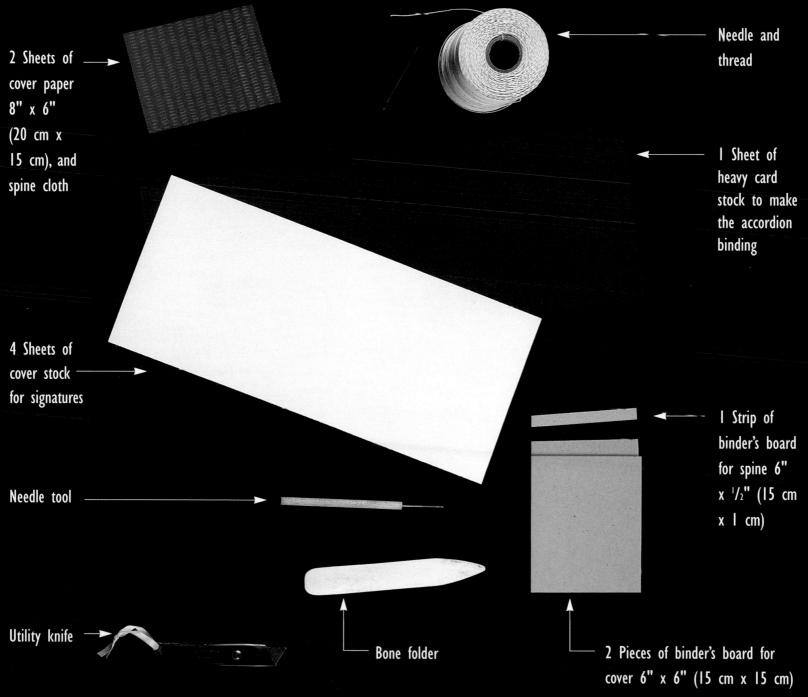

2 Sheets of cover paper 8" x 6" (20 cm x 15 cm), and spine cloth

Needle and thread

1 Sheet of heavy card stock to make the accordion binding

4 Sheets of cover stock for signatures

1 Strip of binder's board for spine 6" x ½" (15 cm x 1 cm)

Needle tool

Utility knife

Bone folder

2 Pieces of binder's board for cover 6" x 6" (15 cm x 15 cm)

1

Fold your signature pages in half. Crease each page with a bone folder. Each signature will have two folded pages or four pages.

2

Use your bone folder to crease your cover paper in half.

3

Beginning at the fold and moving to the right, use your needle to make a series of four marks, ½" (1 cm) apart, at the top and bottom of the paper. With a bone folder and a ruler, crease each segment and fold your accordion. (See How to Make an Illustrated Poem Book for more detailed instructions on folding accordions.)

4

Now you should have a cover paper with three peaks and four valleys in the center. Each of your signatures will fit into the four valleys.

5

Pick up your first signature and place it in your first valley. With your needle tool, punch a hole through the center of both the signature and the cover paper. Then punch a hole 1" (2.5 cm) from the top and 1" (2.5 cm) from the bottom. Do the same thing for the second signature.

6

Cut a piece of thread five times the height of the book, and thread your needle. Push it through the center hole from the cover side, into the center of the first signature. Go down to the bottom hole inside signature one.

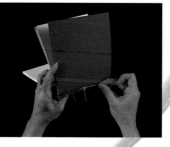

Go out the bottom hole and come in the bottom hole of signature two. Next, go to the inside center hole and come out the back.

Tie the starting tail and your thread together.

Go back into the center hole of the first signature, then up to the top hole. Go out the top hole and into the top hole of the second signature.

Once you are into the second signature, go back down to the center and then come out. Stop here to check that you threaded the signatures with a figure eight.

7

After you have stitched three or four signatures together, trim the pages with a utility knife and cut your cover board to the exact size you desire.

8

Glue your spine board to the center of your spine cloth. Place one cover on each side of the spine. Leave a space between the spine and the cover that is two and a half times the thickness of the binder's board. Glue your decorative papers to the boards so the paper slightly overlaps the cloth.

9

Cut off the corners at a diagonal, then glue and fold the cover paper onto the inside board.

10

Center the sewn concertina inside the covered boards.

11

With a sheet of paper acting as a barrier under your cover page, glue the backside of your cover page to the cover board. Take the barrier out. Close your cover and press.

12

Open your cover and smooth down the inside end sheet with a bone folder. Make sure all the air bubbles have been pressed out. Turn the book over and repeat the process with the other end sheet and cover.

These albums find their
origins in the stitching
of traditional Chinese books and
in Japanese pouch-bound books,
which were made with soft
papers folded in half.

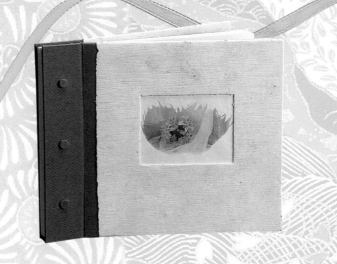

House of Slaves
Gorée Island

Door of No Return
Senegal, W. Africa

Photo Albums

The origins of the Tied-binding Album and the Window-and-post Album can be found in Chinese and Japanese book making; stitching on the outside of the spine was a common way to bind Chinese record-keeping books; Japanese books were made with soft paper that was folded and inserted in the binding so that the folded edge faced away from the spine. The double-thick page prevented the ink on one page from showing through on the next. For the Tied-Binding and the Window-and-Post Album projects shown here, a thick paper is needed to stand up to glue or paste. Both books have covers with visible bindings that imitate Chinese book binding: the spines are stabbed with an awl and tied or sewn around the outside.

Although you can adapt this expandable binding-style for a number of uses—from guest books to sketchbooks—these books are ideal for keeping photographs or mementos. This style of book works well for artists and others who prefer to make the pages of the book first. The flexible bindings free you to design each individual page, and choose the order of pages later. The pacing, and even the amount of material you want to include, can be decided at the end of the project— just before the pages are bound together.

How to Make a Tied-Binding Album

Bits and Pieces

Because these books can be made in any size, measuring pieces the first time out can be daunting. Here are some size relationships, no matter how large or small the book:

- Spine boards are the same height as the cover, and can be as thin as 1" (2.5 cm) or as wide as 4" (10 cm).

- Cut cloth strips—to cover the spine boards—2" (5 cm) longer and wider than the spine board.

- Cut cover paper 2" (5 cm) longer than the height of the book, and the same width as the cover board.

- Cut end papers ¼" (.5 cm) smaller than the cover board.

This project is easy to adapt to make books in different sizes for a variety of purposes; whether keepsake books, photo albums, or guest books. The book covers are binder's board wrapped with cloth and decorative paper. For the interior pages, choose any heavy paper stock: Eighty-pound cover stock is a good weight for making photo albums. You can make a book that has a gatefold spread (an unfolding page that is double the size of the other pages) just by putting the fold of the inside pages on the outside edge of the book, away from the spine, and then trimming a page that would go into the spine.

To decide how large a book to make, first consider the size page you wish to have, then add an inch or two (between 2.5 cm and 5 cm) for the spine. The width of the spine in relation to the cover is a matter of personal taste. The tied-binding style offers many decorative possibilities; try using ribbon, cord, thread, or leather to create different effects.

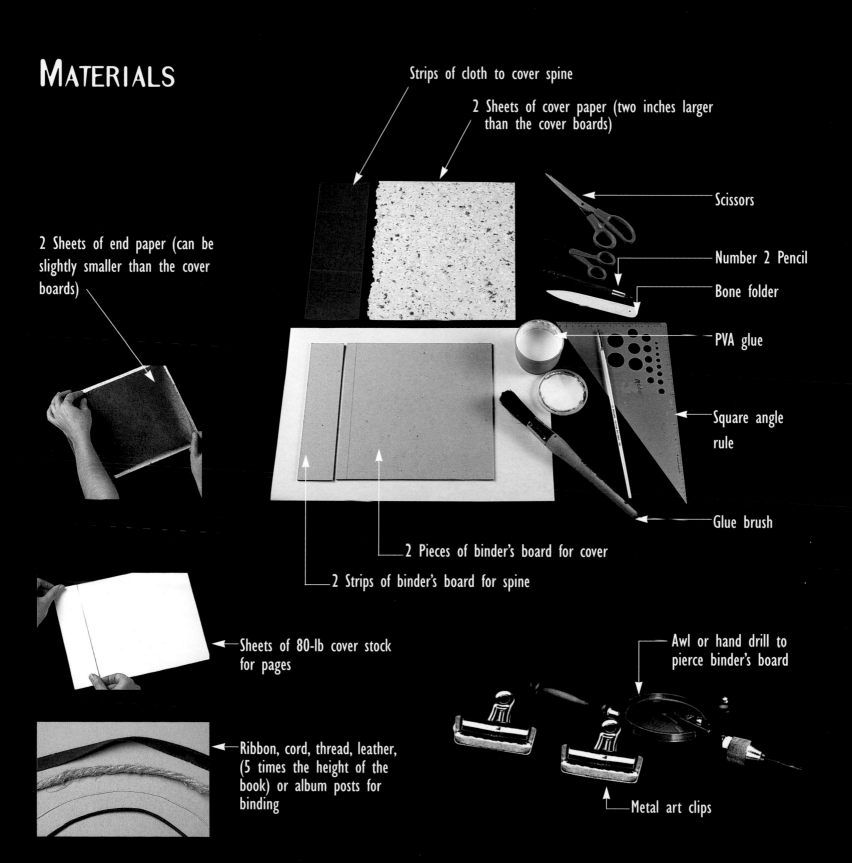

MATERIALS

Strips of cloth to cover spine

2 Sheets of cover paper (two inches larger than the cover boards)

Scissors

Number 2 Pencil

Bone folder

2 Sheets of end paper (can be slightly smaller than the cover boards)

PVA glue

Square angle rule

Glue brush

2 Pieces of binder's board for cover

2 Strips of binder's board for spine

Sheets of 80-lb cover stock for pages

Awl or hand drill to pierce binder's board

Ribbon, cord, thread, leather, (5 times the height of the book) or album posts for binding

Metal art clips

1

Begin by cutting out two strips of board for the spine of the book and two pieces of board for the cover. Cut a strip of cloth (to cover the spine later) 2" (5 cm) longer and wider than the spine board. For the cover, cut two sheets of paper 2" (5 cm) longer than the height of the book and equal to the width of the cover board. Draw a guideline that allows a $^3/_4$" (2 cm) margin along the left side of the cover board.

2

With a glue brush, spread a thin coat of glue quickly and evenly over the entire surface of the cover and spine boards. To help the boards absorb glue, dab all over the surface with the brush after the glue is spread.

3

Place the cloth for the spine on the spine board as shown, so that one edge aligns with the pencil guideline drawn on the cover board. Place the cover paper with one edge slightly overlapping the cloth and press down firmly. To help the glue adhere, rub the entire surface with a bone folder. Look for air pockets and press them out.

4

Flip the book over. Cut the corners of the cloth and cover paper at a diagonal, as shown. Do not cut closer than $1/4$" (.5 cm) from the corners of the cover board. Apply glue along the bottom and along the lip of the spine and the cover board. Working from left to right, use the bone folder to crease the cloth and cover paper up against the lip of the boards. Then fold the material over and press it down firmly. Follow the same procedure for the top edge.

5

Make four shallow cuts along the corners of the spine cloth and cover paper that are not glued down. Fold this surplus material down over the uncovered edges and snip off the triangle peak. Glue the side flaps to the spine and cover board, following the same steps used to glue the top and bottom.

6

Cut out a separate piece of cloth, 2" (5 cm) wide and $1/4$" (.5 cm) shorter than the height of the book. Spread glue evenly on the back of the cloth and press a $3/4$" (2 cm) section on the inside cover, as shown. Fold the spine of the book all the way back and wrap the remainder of the cloth over it. Rub it with a bone folder to help the glue adhere.

7

Cut the paper you have chosen for the end sheet ¼" (.5 cm) smaller than the cover board. Spread glue on the interior of the cover board and then press the end sheet down firmly onto the glue. You may apply the glue on the back side of the paper if you prefer, but placing paper onto glue helps eliminate air bubbles. Repeat steps 1 through 7 to make the back cover. When both covers are complete, flatten them overnight under a weight.

8

To make the interior pages, cut or tear paper ¼" (.5 cm) shorter than the length of the book and ½" (1 cm) shorter than the height of the book. A standard album contains about twenty pages. If you are planning to add photographs or other materials to the album, you will need to add fillers to the spine to make space for them. For the fillers, cut ten to twenty strips of paper that are the same height as the pages and the same width as the spine. Apply a small dab of glue to adhere these strips to the section of the pages that will eventually fit into the spine of the book.

9

Any number of holes can be drilled to make a decorative binding, from two to five—or more. The directions that follow will allow you to bind the book with a simple bootlace stitch. Make a paper template the same size as the spine. Draw a line down the middle of the template, and make five marks an equal distance apart along the line.

10

Collect the pages and place them between the covers. Center pages between the top and bottom covers and make sure they are flush with the spine. Clamp the top and bottom of the spine to hold everything in place.

11

Drill holes in the spine, following the pattern you marked in step 9. If you are working with a hand drill or an electric drill, use a C-clamp to fasten the book to a table. Drill the holes so that they are large enough for the thread or cord to pass through twice. For example, a $^{3}/_{32}$-inch drill bit will make a hole large enough for a $^{1}/_{4}$" (.5 cm) ribbon to pass through twice.

12

Measure and cut a length of ribbon or cord that is five times the height of the book. Push the ribbon through the first hole at the top of the book and pull through until you have a 2" (5 cm) tail on the other side. Keeping the 2" (5 cm) tail in place, spiral the ribbon down through the remaining holes, as shown. When you reach the end, wrap the ribbon around the bottom of the spine and back through the opposite side of the hole you have just exited. Weave the ribbon back to the top. After the last hole, wrap the ribbon around the top of the spine and tie together with the "tail" end.

How to Make a Window-and-Post Album

Bits and Pieces

- Let the image you display in the window influence your decisions concerning the size of the book and the covering you select.

- If you do not like the shiny appearance of aluminum or brass posts, you can cover them like a button with either cloth or paper.

- The post you use must be long enough to go through the front and back cover board and the pages of the book. Posts are sold only in increments of $1/4$" (.5 cm). If the thickness of your book is not a multiple of this, use a post that is shorter rather than taller than your book; a loose post makes an unstable scrapbook.

The Window-and-Post Album is a deluxe version of the Tied-Binding album. Metal posts replace the binding ties, and unscrew easily for adding new pages or making room for bulky keepsakes. The pages remain a heavy, eighty-pound, card stock: Glue invitations, newspaper articles, and ticket stubs directly to the pages, or glue on paper pockets to hold postcards, letters, and fragile souvenirs. The posts fit through the holes made by a standard-size hole-punch and are screwed together. You should use at least three posts to fasten your book.

For a more decorative effect, make a window to display an image on the cover of your book. You can use one of these two methods: With a utility knife, cut away a section of your cover board, and glue the image you want displayed in its place. Another, easier, way to cut cleanly through a thick piece of cardboard is to cut a window into a thin piece of cardboard (such as shirt board), and then attach it to your cover board. Steps 1 through 7 that follow show you how to make this type of window.

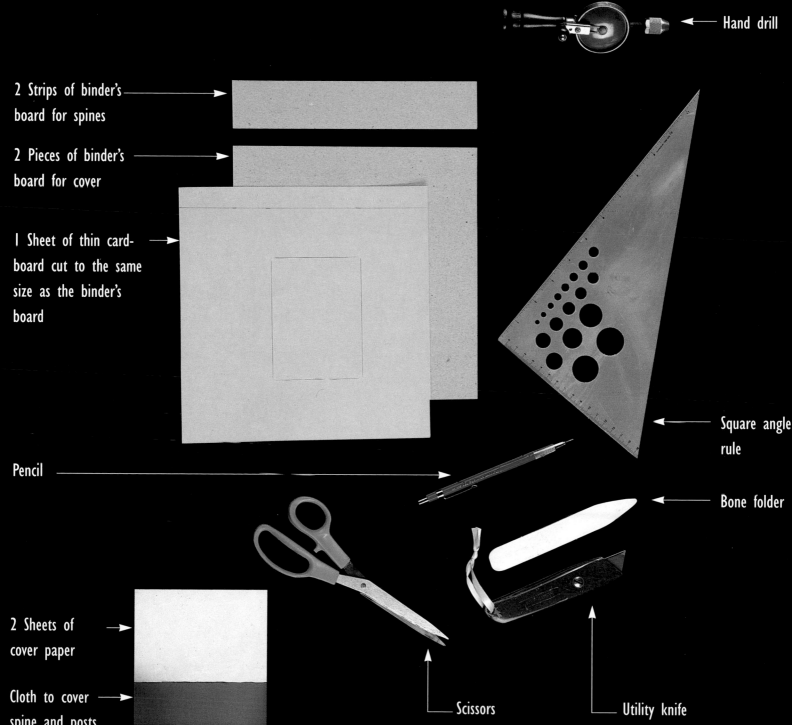

Hand drill

2 Strips of binder's board for spines

2 Pieces of binder's board for cover

1 Sheet of thin card-board cut to the same size as the binder's board

Square angle rule

Pencil

Bone folder

2 Sheets of cover paper

Cloth to cover spine and posts

Scissors

Utility knife

1

Cut a piece of thin cardboard the same size as your cover board. On the thin cardboard, draw the exact size and location of your window. Cut this section out using a utility knife.

2

Draw a ³/₄" (2 cm) margin on the left side of this thin cardboard. Spread glue evenly over the entire surface.

3

Place the cloth for your spine down as shown so that one edge is aligned with the margin. Place the paper you cut for your cover down so that one edge slightly overlaps the cloth. Press the paper and cloth down firmly. Rub the entire surface with a bone folder. Look for air pockets and press them out.

4

Flip this thin cover over and use it as a template to cut out a smaller version of the window from the cover paper. Use scissors to cut diagonal lines from the corners of the smaller window to the corners of the larger window. Fold the four flaps around the edges of the window, then glue them down.

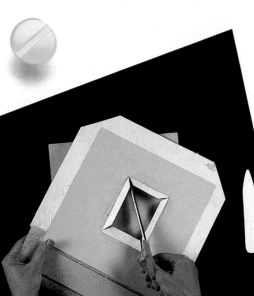

5

Spread glue evenly along the inside edge of the window, and place the image you want displayed face down. Flip the cover over to check the position, then press the image down firmly onto the glue.

6

Spread glue evenly all over the back of the thin cardboard. Next, place the cover board directly on top so that all the edges are aligned. Press the cover board down firmly to make a tight seal. Spread glue on the spine board. Place the spine down on the cloth so it is ¹/₄" (.5 cm) away from the cover board.

7

Flip the book over. Cut the corners of the cloth and cover paper at a diagonal. Do not make the cuts closer than ¼" (.5 cm) from the corners of your cover board. Apply glue along the bottom and along the lip of the spine and cover board. Use the bone folder to crease the cloth and cover paper up against the lip of the boards. Fold the material over and press it down firmly. Follow the same procedure for the top edge.

8

Make a paper template the same size as your spine. Draw a line down the center of the template. Make a mark in the middle, a second mark 1" (2.5 cm) from the top, and a third mark 1" (2.5 cm) from the bottom. Place the paper template on your spine and drill holes in the spine at the three marks on the template. The holes you drill must be wider than the shafts of the album posts.

9

If you wish to cover the posts, cut pieces of cover paper, spine cloth, or another contrasting cloth ⅛" (.3 cm) larger than the head of the album posts. Glue the material to the head of the posts.

10

Use scissors to make several tiny cuts into the material that extend beyond the head of the album posts. Fold and glue this material around the head of the posts.

11

To make the interior pages, follow steps 8 through 11 in the Tied-Binding Album project, but use a larger drill bit—¼" (.5 cm)—to make the holes large enough for the posts. Insert the pages, and place the posts into the holes and screw them together.

A box book acts as a movable, folding sculpture. It can make an exciting diorama for a student's book report. Or it can contain a pop-up figure to surprise and delight.

Box Books

If you combine a beautiful, handmade book with a well-crafted, cloth-covered box, you get a box book. On a practical level, the front and back covers of a book protect the pages. To protect a collection of papers or artwork that needs to be safeguarded but not necessarily bound, you can make a portfolio box for it. The box acts as the cover for the precious material or even as the pages. Hundreds of years ago, artists made portfolio boxes to house their collection of re-lated drawings, lithographs, and small paintings. Following that tradition, Picasso stored prints, depicting bull fighters, in such a box.

Whimsical as well as practical, box books can contain small, three-dimensional scenes or dioramas that pop up when you open the book and fold back neatly into book form when you close it. Popular during the Victorian era, this type of box book can be displayed in a variety of ways, depending on what it contains or how you choose to unfold it.

How to Make an Artist's Portfolio Box

Bits and Pieces

• To keep track of the many separate pieces that make up a portfolio box, it is a good idea to cut and label all the pieces before you assemble them.

• Regardless of the size of your box, the pieces must all fold and overlap properly. Consider the thickness of the boards when determining your final measurements. The right spine should be one board thickness wider than the top and bottom spines. The left spine should be one board thickness wider than the right spine. The left or top board should be large enough to cover all the boards and spines.

• To ensure that the portfolio box can be opened and closed without cracking the spine, crease the interior cloth into the channels between the spines and the cover boards.

This portfolio box is made with five pieces of binder's board that are covered on the outside with cloth and on the inside with complementary decorative paper. Its four sides fold up to accommodate the exact dimensions of your artwork. The top cover of your box, like the cover of a book, can display the title of the work, and be decorated with images to suggest the artwork that is stored inside. This type of box book is ideal if you want to give the viewer the freedom to rearrange the contents.

In this project, you will create a box that will fold to contain artwork that is 7³/₄" (19.5 cm) long and 6¹/₈" (15.5 cm) wide. The box will be ⁵/₈" (1.5 cm) deep. Remember, however, that box books can be tailor-made to fit whatever you want to put inside.

MATERIALS

PVA glue and glue brush

Bone folder

5 Sheets of decorative paper to cover the inside surfaces of the boards

1 Piece of binder's board for top of box

4 Strips of cloth to hinge top, bottom, left, and right spines

1 Piece of binder's board for top spine

1 Piece of binder's board for left spine

1 Piece of binder's board for top cover

1 Piece of binder's board for bottom spine

1 Piece of binder's board for inside cover

1 Piece of binder's board for right spine

1 Piece of cloth 8" x 20" (20 cm x 51 cm)

1 Piece of cloth 23" x 10" (58.5 cm x 25.5 cm)

1 Piece of binder's board for center of base of box

1 Piece of binder's board for bottom of box

1

Cut five boards according to the following dimensions:
Base: 6⁵/₈" (16.5 cm) wide, 8¹/₄" (21 cm) high; Top: 6⁵/₈" (17 cm) wide, 4¹/₈" (10.5 cm) high; Bottom: 6⁵/₈" (17 cm) wide, 4¹/₈" (10.5 cm) high; Right cover: 6⁵/₈" (17 cm) plus the thickness of the board wide. For example, if your board is ¹/₈" (.3 cm) thick, then the total width of your right cover should be 6⁷/₈" (17.5 cm), 8¹/₄" (21 cm) high; Left cover: 6⁵/₈" (17 cm) plus twice the thickness of the board wide, 8¹/₄" (21 cm) plus twice the thickness of the board high.

2

Cut four boards for your spine according to the following dimensions, then arrange the boards as shown. Top spine: 6⁵/₈" (17 cm) wide, ³/₄" (2 cm) high; Bottom spine: 6⁵/₈" (17 cm) wide, ³/₄" (2 cm) high; Right spine: ³/₄" (2 cm) wide plus the thickness of one board, 8¹/₄" (21 cm) high; Left spine ³/₄" (2 cm) plus the thickness of two boards wide, 8¹/₄" (21 cm) plus the thickness of two boards high.

3

Cut a piece of cloth 8" (20 cm) wide and 20" (51 cm) high. Cut another piece of cloth 23" (58.5 cm) wide and 10" (25.5 cm) high.

4

Take your base board and place it in the center of the larger piece of cloth. Use a pencil to outline the base on the inside of the cloth.

5

Draw a straight line from the top corners of the base to the top edge of the cloth. Do the same at the bottom. Cut at an angle from the top edge of the cloth to the corners of the outline as shown. Cut along the line you drew for the top and bottom of the base to remove the two narrow sections of cloth.

6

Place the smaller piece of cloth vertically with the inside facing up. Center the top board and spine, base, and bottom board and spine on the cloth as shown. Leave a $1/8$" (.3 cm) space between each of the boards. Brush a thin layer of glue quickly and evenly over the entire surface of the top board. Press it down firmly on the cloth. Work your way down, gluing one board at a time to the cloth. After the bottom board has been glued, turn the cloth over and rub it with a bone folder to remove air pockets.

Cut the corners of the cloth at a diagonal. Do not cut closer than ¹⁄₄" (.5 cm) from the corner of the top and bottom boards. Apply glue along the sides of the cloth.

Use the bone folder to crease the cloth up against the lip of the boards, then fold the cloth over and press it down firmly. Follow the same procedure to fold and glue the remaining cloth at the top and bottom.

Spread glue on the cloth inside the rectangle base you traced in step 4.

Press the base down firmly on this piece of cloth so that the top and bottom spines fit directly over the two sections of the cloth you removed in step 5. Turn the cloth over and use a bone folder to press out air pockets.

11

Spread a thin coat of glue over the entire surface of the left spine. Press the spine down firmly $1/8$" (.3 cm) away from the base. Adhere the left cover, right spine, and right cover one piece at a time using the same gluing procedure. Leave a $1/8$" (.3 cm) space between the boards. Remove the four corners of the cloth by making a diagonal cut as shown.

12

Glue and fold the edges of the cloth onto the left and right covers.

13

Cut two pieces of cloth, 2" x 6" (5 cm x 15 cm), to use as hinges for your top and bottom spines. Cut two pieces of cloth, 2" x 8" (5 cm x 20 cm), to use as hinges for your left and right spines.

14

Adhere these cloth hinges one at a time. First, glue the inside of the cloth, then center it over the appropriate spine. Press it down firmly. Use a bone folder to press the hinges tightly into the channels between the cover and the spine.

15

Cut five end sheets from a decorative paper to cover the insides of the boards. End sheets for the top and bottom boards should be 6" (15 cm) wide and 3½" (9 cm) high. End sheets for the left and right cover and the base should be 6" (15 cm) wide and 8" (20 cm) high. Spread a thin layer of glue on the backside of each sheet and press them down firmly on the boards. Use a bone folder to press out air pockets or wrinkles.

16

Place the contents of your book on the base. Fold the top and bottom sections of the box over the contents. Fold the right board, then the left board, to close the box.

How to Make a Pop-Up Box Book

During the Victorian era, it was popular to use paper and cardboard to make doll houses, farmyards, parks, and other settings. Many of these scenes even contained movable parts; doors opened and closed, figures moved amidst the scenery, gates swung open, making them captivating toys for children. These three-dimensional displays were quite elaborate, yet they could be folded and stored neatly in book form.

In this project, a simplified version of a Victorian pop-up scene, you will make a book that unfolds to reveal a 5" (13 cm) box with two windows that is ideal for displaying a small paper sculpture.

Bits and Pieces

- If you choose to make a book box in a different size from the one assembled here, remember to consider the thickness of the interior and exterior boards. For the book to fold properly, the interior boards must be slightly smaller and thinner than the two exterior cover boards. The space between the two cover boards must be equal to their thickness plus the total thickness of the interior boards.

- When you adhere the hinges, be sure that they are placed close to the edge of the cover board, not on the lip. If one interior board overlaps another, its hinge should be a bit wider.

- To prevent warping, put the book under pressure immediately after you finish making it.

MATERIALS

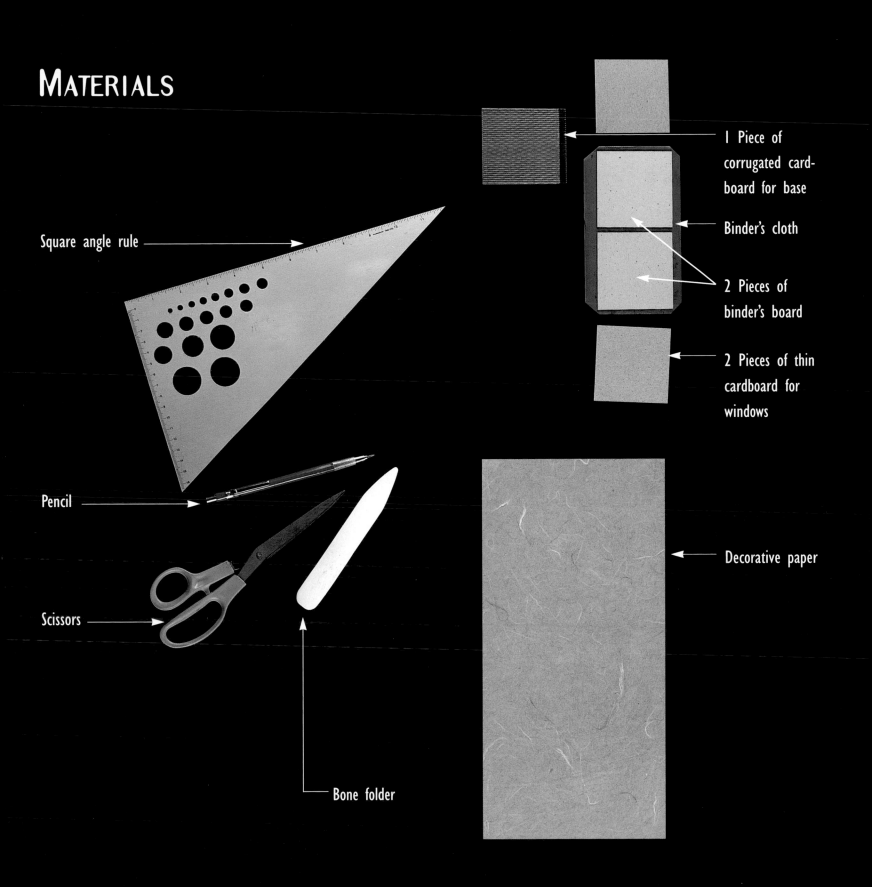

Square angle rule

1 Piece of corrugated card-board for base

Binder's cloth

2 Pieces of binder's board

2 Pieces of thin cardboard for windows

Pencil

Scissors

Bone folder

Decorative paper

1

Cut two pieces of binder's board 5" (13 cm) wide and 5" (13 cm) high. From shirt board (thin card-board), cut two pieces for your windows that measure 4³/₄" (12 cm) wide and 4³/₄" (12 cm) high. From cardboard or thick paper, cut a board for the base of your box that measures 4³/₄" (12 cm) wide and 5¹/₄" (13 cm) high. Cut a piece of cloth 12" (30.5 cm) wide and 6¹/₂" (16 cm) high.

2

Spread a thin layer of glue over the entire surface of the two 5" x 5" (13 cm x 13 cm) boards. Press them firmly onto the inside of the cloth, leaving a ¹/₄" (.5 cm) space between the boards. Remove the corners by making a diagonal cut. Do not cut closer than ¹/₄" (.5 cm) from the corners of the board. Flip the cloth and boards over, then use a bone folder to press out air pockets.

3

Apply glue along the thin section of cloth that extends beyond the bottom of the boards. Working from left to right, use the bone folder to crease the cloth up against the lip of the boards. Fold the cloth over and press it down firmly. Follow the same procedure to adhere the cloth extending beyond the top and sides.

4

On each piece of shirt board, use an angle to draw a square 2" (5 cm) smaller than the board. To center this square properly, make each side 1" (2.5 cm) away from the sides of the shirt board. Use a mat knife and a ruler to cut out this smaller square to make a window.

5

Cut two pieces of decorative paper each 5½" (13.5 cm) high and 11" (30 cm) long. Glue one window to one side of the decorative paper so that a ¾" (2 cm) margin exists around three sides. Use a razor to cut out a smaller version of the window from the decorative paper. With scissors, cut diagonal lines from the corners of this window to the corners of the window in the shirt board.

6

Place a ruler along the top of the shirt board. Draw a straight line across the top of the paper. Follow the same procedure to draw a line across the bottom of the decorative paper. Cut one line as shown until you reach the shirt board. Then make a cut to remove this strip. Follow the same procedure to remove the other section of paper.

7

Use a bone folder to crease the four flaps of paper around the inside edges of the window, then glue them down. Next, apply glue along the three narrow sides of decorative paper that extend beyond the shirt board. Fold the paper over and press it down firmly onto the frame of the window.

8

Fold the window you have just wrapped down on the remainder of the decorative paper. Use a pencil to trace the window onto the paper. Cut out the square you have drawn.

If you want to cover the window with a piece of mylar or acetate, spread glue around the frame of the window as shown. Press the mylar or acetate down firmly onto the frame.

10

Apply glue onto the frame of the other window, and fold it over so both windows are square. Rub the frame with a bone folder to press out air pockets.

11

Glue the narrow strip of decorative paper that extends beyond the window frame to either the right or left side of the cover board. Rub this strip with a bone folder to press out wrinkles.

12

Follow steps 1 through 11 to make the window for the other side of your book.

13

Score and fold a ½" (1 cm) section from the top of the base board. With this section folded, the base now becomes a square. Spread glue on this ½" (1 cm) section and press it firmly onto the bottom of one of your boards.

14

Cut a piece of paper or cloth 10¼" (26 cm) wide and 4⅞" (12.5 cm) high. Spread a thin layer of glue on the side of this material that you do not want exposed, and place it over the two inside boards as shown. Use a bone folder to press the paper tightly into the space between the cover board and to remove wrinkles or air pockets.

New Directions: Trends and Traditions

Whether they are art books, journals, scrapbooks, photo albums, or box books, handmade books are a personal, tactile way of communicating to the reader. Techniques that are common from one book type to another make it easy to link styles and create such ingenious books as the scroll, accordion with pamphlet, and extended accordion books described in this section. Contemporary book artists demonstrate how to extend these book forms to express their art while establishing an intimate relationship with the viewer.

The book artists represented in this section use traditional bookmaker's tools and materials along with the most sophisticated technology of our modern era to create precious one-of-a-kind or limited edition books. They are artists trained in other fields who have adapted many of the book-making styles and techniques to create new and beautiful book designs. For them, making books is not only a way to communicate what they perceive—it also represents an opportunity to help others understand what a book is, and what it can become.

How to Make a Scroll

The choice of materials can determine the structural form of a book. The best materials to use for a scroll book, a rolled sheet of paper or cloth, are those that resist folding or cutting; historically, in China, silk was rolled into scrolls because it rolled easily and was more difficult to cut; certain vellums are best used and stored rolled, not folded. Although the scroll is an ancient book form, contemporary artists continue to use this form when they want to display an entire image all at once.

The following steps describe how to make a scroll book with flexible paper and with one dowel cut flush to the height of the paper. Trim the dowel using a utility knife. Anything cylindrical can substitute for the dowel—pencils, cardboard tubing, even straws.

1

You will need one or two dowels, pliable paper, and ribbon or string to tie it.

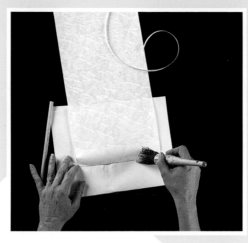

2

Spread glue on the edge of the paper that will be rolled around the dowel.

3

Roll the glued portion of paper tightly around the dowel.

4

At the other end of the paper, about ¹/₂" (1 cm) away from the edge, cut two slits parallel to the paper's edge, ¹/₄" (.5 cm) apart. Starting from the outside of the scroll, thread the ribbon through the lower slit, then through the upper slit back to the outside of the scroll. Thread the ribbon through so that the edge of the ribbon is hidden.

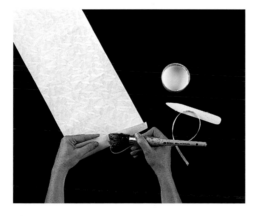

5

Glue a small amount of the end of the ribbon to the underside of the rest of the ribbon.

Deborah Davidson uses the scroll format in her book *Voices*.

How to Make an Accordion with Pamphlet Insert

An accordion can be folded in many different ways to create pages in a variety of widths. It is used as part of the spine in a concertina binding. If the folded pages of the accordion are large enough, a signature or pamphlet can be stitched into one of the folds as a small subsection of the book.

For additional pages, it is easy to sew in another, matching, signature in the second fold.

 1

Using heavy weight paper, construct a four-panel accordion fold following steps 1 through 3 in How to Make an Illustrated Poem Book. Fold two sheets of lighter weight paper, cut to a size slightly smaller than one panel of the accordion, into a signature. Place the signature in one valley of the accordion. Use a needle to make three evenly spaced holes through both the crease of the signature and the valley of the accordion.

 2

Cut a section of thread two times the height of the signature. Thread the needle and begin to stitch the pages together by going through the center hole. Go up through the top hole, then down through the bottom hole. Go back out the center hole.

Suzanne Moore uses this technique in *We Belong to the Earth*, where a pamphlet page is sewn into the center fold of the accordion.

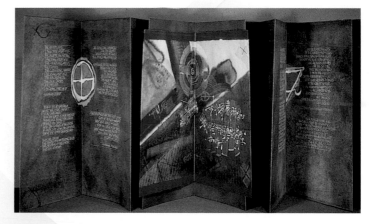

3

Tie off the ends of the thread by making a double knot. Cut off any excess thread.

How to Make an Extended Accordion

Book pages are often made by folding a single sheet of paper in half, with the fold positioned at the binding edge. A gate fold is an extended page made by folding the outside edge of an extra long page back into the center fold. As a result, a gate fold opens twice to reveal two pages instead of one. To make the double gate fold shown here, fold each sheet of paper in half and then fold each half into the center. A double gate fold can be opened twice to a spread of four pages. If you stitch together a number of gate folds, you begin to form an accordion. Use heavier weight paper, such as print-making paper or cover stock, for the pages of such accordion books. To protect the pages and finish off the book, attach binder's board covered with paper or cloth to the outside panels of the accordion.

1

Cut four sheets of paper 24" (61 cm) wide and 6" (15 cm) high. If you want to make a book that is larger or smaller, remember that in order for it to end with a square, the width of the paper should be four times the height.

2

Fold the width of each sheet into quarters. Use a bone folder to make a sharp crease.

3

Unfold and place two sheets one on top of the other so that they fold away from each other. With a piece of thread that is twice the height of the paper and a needle, sew the two sheets together at the first fold using a three-hole pamphlet stitch (described in detail in the Journals and Scrapbooks section). Sew the other two sheets together in the same way.

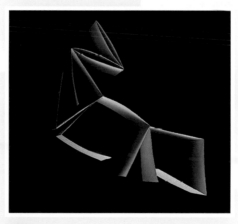

In *Quilters and Weavers*, four gate folds are stitched together to create an accordion that opens up to form four cubes.

4

With each pair of sheets laid one on top of the other, take the top sheet of one sewn section and the top sheet of the other sewn section and join them together at their center folds using a three-hole pamphlet stitch.

5

Stand the book upright. Position the pages so that each sheet makes a square. To close the book, close each gate fold first, then collapse the four sections together like an accordion.

Gallery of Artists

Laura Blacklow
Last Two Weeks in August
4" x 3¹/₂" (10.2 cm x 8.9 cm)
Accordion fold with Polaroids

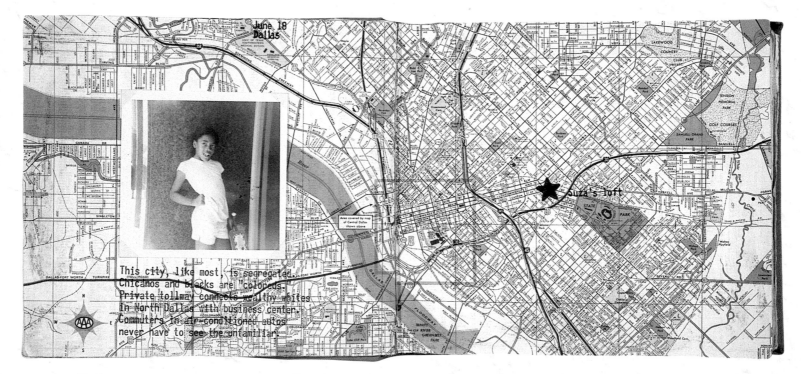

Laura Blacklow
Territories
8" x 8" (20.3 cm x 20.3 cm)
Collage: map, color photograph, stick-on star, type

Laura Blacklow
The Disappeared
11" x 17" (27.9 cm x 43.2 cm)
Mixed media, text (Braille, English, Spanish)

Laura Blacklow
Altar Piece for Gary
11" x 8¹⁄₂" (27.9 cm x 21.6 cm)
Accordion fold book, Van Dyke brown print, pastels

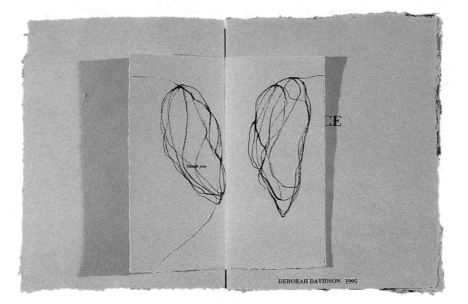

Deborah Davidson
Voce
11" x 9" (27.9 cm x 22.9 cm)
Variable edition
Handmade papers, ink, monotype

Deborah Davidson
Voce (Detail)

Deborah Davidson
Trace (Detail)

Deborah Davidson
Trace
168" x 72" (426.8 cm x 182.8 cm)
Mixed media, handmade papers

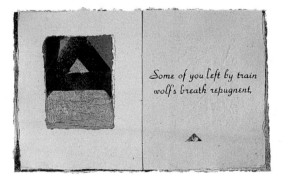

Some of you left by train
wolf's breath repugnant,

Deborah Davidson
Family Tree
20" x 16" (50.8 cm x 40.6 cm)
Handmade paper, monotype, Lettraset

Nancy Leavitt
The Desert Speaks: Book Two
13" x 5 ¼" x 1" (33 cm x 13.3 cm x 2.5 cm)
Gouache painting and lettering, handmade muslin paper,
cloth binding

Nancy Leavitt
The Desert Speaks: Book Two
(Detail)

Nancy Leavitt
A Green Journey
12" x 10" x 1" (30.5 cm x 25.4 cm x 2.5 cm)
Gouache painting and lettering on dyed and
paste-prepared handmade papers

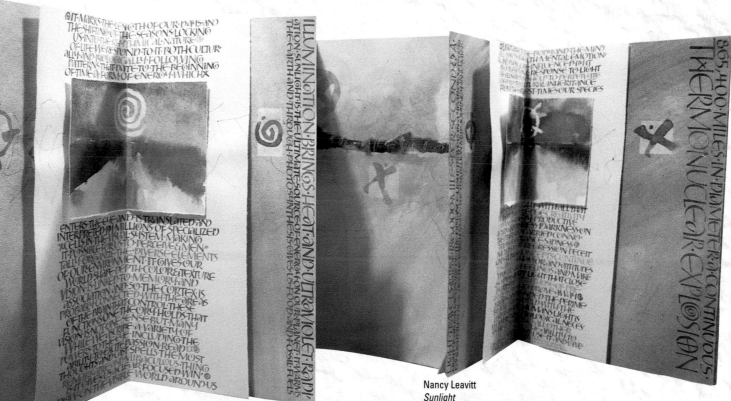

Nancy Leavitt
Sunlight
12½" x 8½" x ½" (31.8 cm x 21.6 cm x 1.3 cm)
Gouache painting and lettering on paste-papered Arches text

Angela Lorenz
Pandora's Book
6" x 8" x 6" (15.2 cm x 20.3 cm x 15.2 cm)
Paper, buttons, haberdashery

Angela Lorenz
An Eye for An Eye (Closed)
1³/₄" (4.4 cm) diameter
Etching on vellum

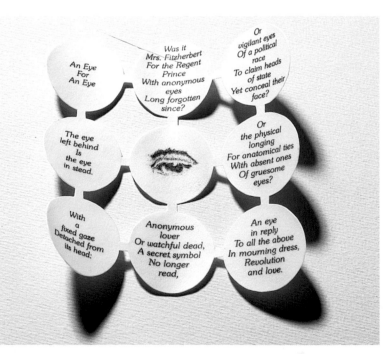

Angela Lorenz
An Eye for An Eye (Open)

Angela Lorenz
Paper Plates. She's a Dish
16" x 16" (40.6 cm x 40.6 cm)
Spaghetti collograph and letterpress

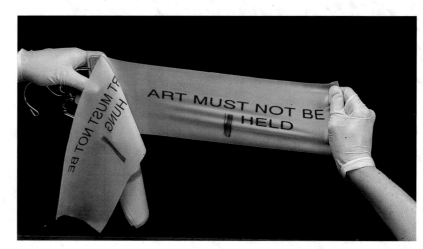

Angela Lorenz
Laytext
8" x 15" (20.3 cm x 38.1 cm)
Screen print on Latex; skirt hanger,
canvas, zipper

Angela Lorenz
Paper Plates. She's a Dish (Cover detail)

Angela Lorenz
Laytext (Cover detail)

Mary McCarthy
Rhythms
11" x 11⅝" (27.9 cm x 29.5 cm)
Opens to 40" (101.6 cm)
Collage, side-sewn with multiple spreads

Mary McCarthy
The Overseer
8½" x 6" x 1½" (21.6 cm x 15.2 cm x 3.8 cm)
Box book, collage/paper

Mary McCarthy
Feel the Rapture
9" x 2" x 1½" (22.9 cm x 5.1 cm x 3.8 cm)
Opens to 13" (33 cm)
Collage, handmade papers, and ink, accordion
fold with box

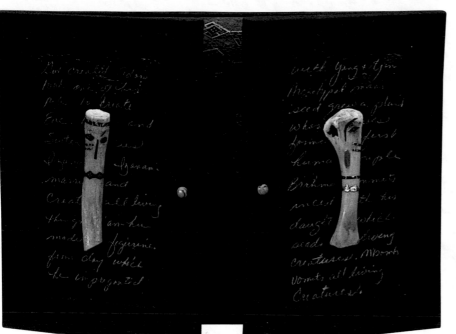

Mary McCarthy
Harmonious Union
7" x 9 ³/₄" x ¹/₂"
(17.8 cm x 24.8 cm x 1.3 cm)
Collage, bone figure

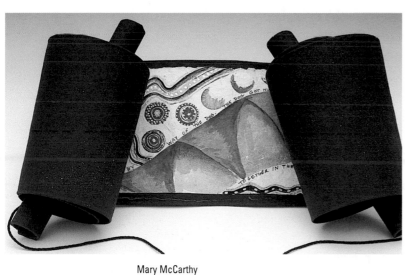

Mary McCarthy
A Bad Rap
6" x 6" (15.2 cm x 15.2 cm)
Scroll, gouache, and ink on handmade paper

Mary McCarthy
4 Winds
8 ¹/₂" x 8 ¹/₈" (21.6 cm x 20.6 cm)
Handmade paper collage, accordion fold

Suzanne Moore
Alphabetical Collection (Interior)

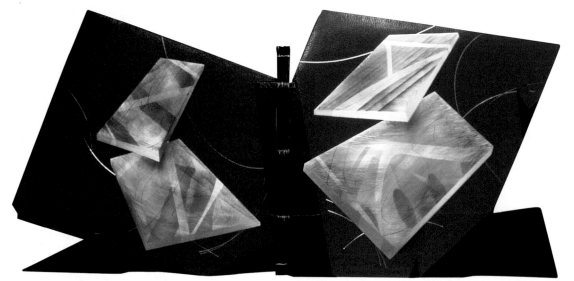

Suzanne Moore
Alphabetical Collection
Binding by Donald Glaister
10¹/₄" x 22" (26 cm x 55.9 cm)
Binding: Moroccan leather, painted aluminum, and tooling
Pages: Gouache and gold leaf on Rives BFK

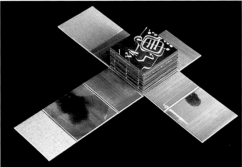

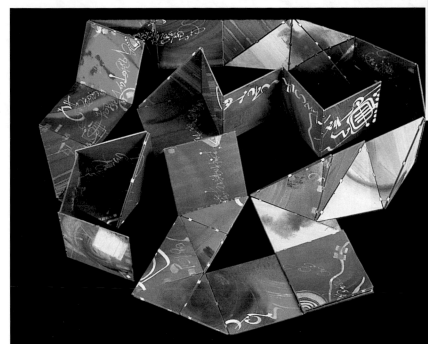

Suzanne Moore
A Maze in Book (Three dimensional form and folded)
Binding design by Daniel Kelm
35" (88.9 cm) laid out
Unique copy, wire-bound folding book

Suzanne Moore
Animal Dreams (Interior)
Gouache and ink on handmade paper
Binding by Donald Glaister
9⅝" x 7¼" (24.5 cm x 18.4 cm)
Binding: Moroccan leather with oak insets and vellum buttons

Nancy Natale
Souvenir of Maine
6" x 6¹/₄" (15.2 cm x 15.8 cm)
Opens to 12" x 12" (30.5 cm x 30.5 cm)
Monotype collage on board

Nancy Natale
Perhaps
13" x 39" (33 cm x 99.1 cm)
Monotype collage

Nancy Natale
Ancestor Icon
25" x 13" x 5" (63.5 cm x 33 cm x 12.7 cm)
Open monotype collage, wood construction

Nancy Natale
X Marks the Spot
12" x 98" (30.5 cm x 249 cm)
Monotype collage on wood

Resources

The Bookbinder's Warehouse, Inc.
31 Division Street
Keyport, NJ 07735
908-264-0306

Charrette
31 Olympia Avenue
Woburn, MA 01888
800-500-0278

Daniel Smith
4150 First Avenue South
Seattle, WA 98124-5568
800-426-6740

Dick Blick
P.O. Box 1267
Galesburg, IL 61402
800-447-8192

Harcourt Bindery
51 Melcher Street
Boston, MA 02210
617-542-5858

Jessica Wrobel (marbled papers and
    cloth)
186 Bachelor Street
West Newbury, MA 01985
508-363-2106

Johnson's Bookbinding Supplies
32 Trimountain Avenue
P.O. Box 280
South Range, MI 49963
906-487-9522

Kate's Paperie
561 Broadway
New York, NY 10012
212-941-9816

Light Impressions
P.O. Box 940
Rochester, NY 14603-0940
800-828-6216

Paper Sources
232 West Chicago Avenue
Chicago, IL 60610
312-337-0798

Pearl Art and Crafts
579 Mass. Avenue
Cambridge, MA 02139
617-547-6600

Rugg Road Papers
105 Charles Street
Boston, MA 02114
617-742-0002

Talas
568 Broadway
New York, NY 10012
212-736-7744

Talin Book Bindery
947 Rt. 6A
Yarmouthport, MA 02675
508-362-8144

University Products, Inc.
P.O. Box 101
517 Main Street
Holyoke, MA 01041
800-336-4847

Suggested Readings

Diehl, Edith. *Bookbinding: Its Background and Techniques.* New York: Dover Publications, 1980.

Ikegami, Kojiro. *Japanese Bookbinding: Instructions from a Master Craftsman.* New York: Weatherhill, Inc., 1986.

Johnson, Arthur W. *The Thames and Hudson Manual of Bookbinding.* London: Thames and Hudson, Ltd, 1978.

Johnson, Pauline. *Creative Bookbinding.* New York: Dover Publications, 1990.

Laplantz, Shereen. *Cover to Cover.* California: Lark Books, 1994.

Lewis, A. W. *Basic Bookbinding.* New York: Dover Publications, 1957.

Smith, Keith. *Non-Adhesive Binding: Books Without Paste or Glue.* New York: Sigma Foundation, Inc., 1991.

————. *Structure of the Visual Book.* New York: Visual Studies Workshop Press, 1984.

Zeir, Franz. *Books, Boxes, and Portfolios.* New York: Design Press, 1990.

contributors

Laura Blacklow
215 Eire Street
Cambridge, MA 02139
617-492-2054

Illuminated Persian and Medieval manuscripts combined with memories of the colorfully illustrated books of her childhood inspire Laura Blacklow to create her own visually enticing books.

Deborah Davidson
1 Fitchburg Street #311
Somerville, MA 02143
617-666-3674

Deborah Davidson often uses her family history as a subject for her books to remember and pay homage to it. Her artist's books are the most formal yet the most personal of her work, giving voice and form to her experience.

Nancy Leavitt
P.O. Box 330
Stillwater, ME 04489
207-827-6088

Nancy Leavitt creates books that are contemporary versions of manuscripts produced during the fifth through the fifteenth century. Her work, which is influenced by historical alphabets and manuscripts, and children's language, explores lettering as a symbol, combining lettering and painting into one image.

Angela Lorenz
Casella Postale 394
40100 Bologna, Italy
011-39-51-222174

Travel is an inherent part of Angela Lorenz's research. Her investigations into cultures, habits, and traditions lead to mixed-media creations that sometimes resemble books.

Mary McCarthy
45 Tremlett Street
Dorchester, MA 02124
617-265-6156

Mary McCarthy's work is rooted in religious, mythological, and philosophical themes. Using handmade papers, collage, and various printing techniques, she often blends rituals from a variety of cultures to evoke a more universal understanding.

Suzanne Moore
P.O. Box 477
Brown Road
Ashfield, MA 01330
413-625-6659

with: Donald Glaister   Daniel Kelm
        P.O. Box 477   1 Cottage Street
        Brown Road   Box 449
        Ashfield, MA 01330   Easthampton, MA 01027
        413-625-6659   413-527-8044

Suzanne Moore's books interpret a range of subjects, from gardening to Sequoyah and his Cherokee alphabet. Historic illuminated manuscripts, the paintings of Vermeer and Kandinsky, and the wonder of the natural world all inspire her contemporary books.

Nancy Natale
25 Curtis Street
W. Somerville, MA 02144
617-625-5807

Nancy Natale is drawn to making artwork in book form by the desire to discover and communicate history. She is also drawn by the challenge of blending the real with the imaginary in order to more closely examine what is real.